Do You Want to Be a Slave?

A Message to Troubled Youth in America

Jonah Sanders

Death is nothing, but to live defeated is to die every day.

-Napoleon Bonaparte

Contents

Acknowledgment

With some authors placing so much time trying to figure out who they wish to thank, I thought about it with the same intensity, but only can name a few, those being my grandmother Mrs. Alease Sanders, Hazel Horne, Cierra Simmons and Special Thanks to Don Blakely.

Forward

First and foremost, I wish to thank you; the young man or young woman who has taken the time out of their busy schedule to read this book. I'm rather sure that you would prefer being on Facebook, Instagram, or one of the other popular social media sites, so I appreciate your time. Now, you may be wondering from the title as to what I'm getting at, so to place your mind at ease; no, I'm not asking you if you want to be a slave, but rather presenting how you can and will become a slave due to irrational actions.

You may not believe that slavery exists today, in which most people don't, but it is a strong as ever. It's not the same as the Atlantic Slave Trade, in which Africans were enslaved and shipped to the shores of America; the slavery that I'm presenting is much worst: that being; becoming a slave to yourself through ignorance. For every time you do something ignorant and idiotic you sell yourself into slavery. Then, if you didn't know, under the 13th Amendment of the United States Constitution it clearly states that you can sell yourself into slavery by committing crimes.

Amendment XIII [1865]

Section 1. Neither slavery nor involuntary servitude, except as a punishment for a crime wherefore the party shall have been duly convicted, shall exist within the United States....

Now, you may be wondering as to my intention for writing this, so to be direct, its because I care. I was exactly where you're at now. I was lost and mad at the world as well. I felt neglected. I felt hopeless.

With me being in prison for as long as I have, I wanted to share my life with you so that you can see what will become of you unless you take control over the mental, spiritual, and physical aspects of yourself. So, hopefully... you take control of your life.

Jonah Sanders

The Crime & Before

The value of a thing sometimes lies not in what one attains with it but in what one pays for it – what it cost us.

-Friedrich Nietzsche

The Crime & Before

The actual date of my crime was July 7th, 2004, but with the intention of painting a clear picture of my mind state and overall situation, I'll begin with the day previous. So, on July 6th, 2004, I was laying on the tan carpet of an abandoned apartment in a complex on Roswell Road in the City of Atlanta, Ga. Between eating sunflower seeds and oatmeal pies, I was trying to formulate a plan to come up out of the hole that I had feel into. With me just getting out of county jail for a frivol burglary charge, I was flat broke, frightened, and pissed off at myself. I wondered how I had went from being on a high horse to... nothing. Maybe I was just delusional with my reality.

With my back sore from the hard floor, I sat up and looked around the empty apartment. The only things that were in the room with me were a few items that I had stolen from one of the houses around the corner: a small television, DVD player, and a tote bag. Entertainment ruled my every minute; odd how I even entertained myself at my lowest. Sick of eating sunflower seeds, my stomach rumbled for some real food. If I'm not mistaken, I had eaten a hamburger the day before, but that would have been it except for traditional junk food. Rising to my feet, I stalked back and forth trying to think of something that I could do to get some money. Then, I wasn't looking for a bunch of it either, just enough to get a meal.

Jonah Sanders

I knew a few people that I could have gotten some drugs from, but my heart couldn't take it anymore. I didn't want to destroy someone's life like that. I can remember looking in this one junkie's eyes and seeing a void that scared me, it was as if she didn't even have soul, as if she was one of the walking dead that are depicted in zombie movies. I could tell that she was once beautiful, but the drugs had destroyed her. Starring into her eyes, all I could see was pain and humiliation. So, drugs were out of the equation for me.

Pacing back and forth I tried to think of something – anything! Robbery was out of the question because I just wasn't into that. I didn't want to take something from someone by force. I wasn't soft, but deep down inside of me, I just couldn't fathom that. I knew of guys who did stick-ups and would just shoot a person before they demanded the money. I honestly felt that it was idiotic to do, because if the person didn't have any money than they were just shot for nothing. It may seem odd, but the whole robbery thing was heinous to me.

Sad as it sounds, but with every possible thing that I could think of to make some quick money, why did my mind go back to burglary?

The Crime & Before

Even though I had just got out of county jail for doing so, I guess I assumed that it was the lesser if two evils because I could just break in and take a few things then go on about my business without anyone getting hurt. All I would have to do is walk around the house lined streets and check to see if the owner was at work or whatever. Once I peeped a house that didn't have a security sticker, I would just have to walk around about five or six times to get a feel of the environment then get to it.

Coming to what seemed to be the most logical choice (yeah, I know), I looked through the blinds and saw that it was night. Cleaning up the crumbs and other evidence that I had in the apartment, I hurried out the door to my mission. Walking through the complex, I kept my head down as I moved with the shadows. I felt as if I was some type of big cat; a panther or a jaguar on the hunt for its prey. On the sidewalk of the house lined streets, I whistled in an attempt to fit into my surroundings.

Making my way up and down the streets I spotted two target homes. One was a red brick home at the corner of the block, while the other was a Victorian home with a screened patio. Picking the first because it was the most secluded, I went along whistling about with my hands in my pants pockets. Not noticing a security sticker, I rung the door bell then waited for someone to answer.

After a few minutes and no one answering, I glanced around at the other homes, went back to whistling and waited a little more. Moving to the side of the home, I shouted, "What the! Come on, man!" as I saw the security sticker. Good ol' ADT. I couldn't do anything, but shake my head.

Then as I looked inside of the kitchen window and seeing some bagels on the stand I almost lost it. "Bagels? This is crazy," I mumbled to myself as my mouth salivated. The sight of the bagels alone made me want to still break in and seize them. The owner had to be teasing me! My stomach was doing all type of twist and turns now.

Getting myself under control, I moved on to the other home. Checking the sides and back of the home, I was sure that it was free of any security stickers, so I was in the game. Popping one of the side windows I crawled inside. From what I could tell, the home was of good people, because it gave off a peaceful aura. Instantly, I felt terrible because I was disturbing the peace of someone's home, but my stomach was moving me now and all reason was gone.

Going straight to the kitchen I ransacked the cabinets in search for food. Making myself something to eat, I then placed some food in bag and moved along the home.

The Crime & Before

 In the living room I peeped the electronics as I tried to figure out how I would move the stuff and who I could sell it to. Hearing the phone ring, I jumped out of my skin as I was terrified of getting caught. Rushing back to the window in which I had crawled in through I was about to leave until I stopped myself short of it and brushed off the fear as I mumbled to myself, "It's just the phone."

With the answering machine picking up, I heard a child thank, who I assume was the owner of the home, for taking her to the skating rink the other day and how she could hardly wait to see them again. Disgusted with myself, I crawled back out of the window to walk in the lonely night.

Later, early the next morning, I woke up with a scheme. I figured that if I could just hit one good lick that I could just give it all up and begin fresh. Washing my face, I hurried off into the darkness of the one A.M morning, up the road to a section of town that was called "Little Mexico". At my destination I looked for a Mexican that I knew, but couldn't find him. My plan was to try to work a deal on some cars because all I would have to do was steal three or four then drop them off. It would give me enough money to pay for a room for a few months, some food and time to think.

Frustrated, I walked back down the road, but stopped short of my dwelling and made my way into an apartment complex that had a lot of criminal activity. Seeing a few people that I knew, I kicked it with a guy who eventually asked me if I committed burglaries. With this being a collection of street people, I told him that I did, then he suggested that we do something together. Needing the money, I immediately agreed and asked when he wanted to do something. He must have been hurting just as much as myself, because he wanted to do something then. Not thinking about the consequences, I got into his car and sat back as we rode around looking for an easy target. Something deep inside of me told me to get out of the car, but the feeling of desperation overwhelmed me.

So, as we rode around on July 7th, 2004, we eventually stopped at target home in a cul-de-sac. Believing that no one was inside, we both got out of the car and made our way to the home. Going to the side of the house, we popped the window and climbed in. With me going in first, he passed me the gun and told me to hold it. With the both of us inside we walked to a door to the right of the window that we had climbed through and opened it.

Everything changed terribly when the door was opened, and I saw a woman and her child, frightened and confused, I raised the gun and told her not to move. She wasn't supposed to be inside the home, no one was. The guy that was with me took over and locked her in the room. With us already inside, he came up with the idea that we just go upstairs and get what we can, then get out as quick as possible. (Yeah, I know). Like an idiot I followed behind him up the stairs. On the top floor he went one way while I went the other. (SMH)

I opened the first door that I came across and saw a woman getting ready for work. Now, scared witless, I raised the gun and told her not to move. Hearing my voice, the guy I was with ran inside of the room and freaked out. Asking if anyone else was inside of the home, he then ushered the daughters into the mothers' room. The woman pleaded that she wouldn't call the police if we just left, but I couldn't move due to the fear of what would come if we were caught.

The guy that I was with suggested that we take the woman to the bank and withdraw some money. I was so gone I just went along with everything.

Before leaving he put the younger children in the room with the lady and child that we first saw, then had the mother and her oldest daughter get into the SUV as he

Jonah Sander

got into the driver seat and I sat in the back with the gun. Riding to the bank I was in a void, I didn't know what was going on anymore… I was just there. No one was supposed to be home.

Arriving at the bank, the lady got out to go withdraw the money, but the bank wasn't open yet. Looking around fearfully, she made her way back to the SUV when a cop suddenly tried to sneak up on the driver's side as the guy that I was with pulled off. Speeding off, the guy that I was with drove to an apartment complex down the road. Jumping out of the SUV we ran inside of an apartment with the woman's daughter running beside us. (Weird right?) I ran inside one of the bedroom then got under the bed. You may laugh, but I didn't know what to do, especially when I heard helicopters and saw infrared beams hit the walls.

Being Arrested & Taken to the County Jail

Is it possible to get up even after the hardest fall?

-Jonah Sanders

Being Arrested & Taken to Jail

When the officers first came into the apartment then into the bedroom where I was hiding I thought that I had gotten away because the officers walked in then left back out. But, within a few minutes, the same officers came back into the room and dragged me from under the bed. I'm sure many of you are wondering as to why I even hid under the bed, but I'll ask you this: where else was I to hide? I was scared to death and believed that I would have been shot and killed just to be an example for all those who robbed and did crime. Handcuffed, I was ushered outside.

It was pandemonium. It seemed as if all the cities news crews had their cameras out recording. I tried to hide my face but a few of them still got good shots. Placed in the back seat of the squad car I sat with my head down. I don't know if it was because I felt ashamed as to what I had just done or because I was hiding my face from the flashes of the cameras; it was likely a combination of both, because no one wants to be seen when they are in a state of humiliation.

Peeping up from my humbled head I watched as residents came out of their apartments pointing my way as they spoke amongst each other. I believe that it is funny how people are drawn to others hardships. If we looked at it for what it was we would see that its been going on since the beginning of time. Just look at some of the videos or pictures of public punishment, such as hangings and you'll likely see a huge crowd just lounging around watching as if it were a base carnival event. The most known instance would be when Christ was crucified; you'll see a huge crowd.

Over the years I've contemplated this, yet still can't understand it. At times I believe that Darwin was correct in, humans evolving from animals. Why would anyone want to watch another suffer? I tell you what, if you think that you have a rational explanation let me know because I give up trying to figure it out.

I assume that the officers got tired of the media too because they finally got inside, hit the lights, then pulled off. As we rode to what I believed would be the County Jail. I sat in silence as I watched everyone watch me in the backseat. Funny as it may be, but I even had a young girl wave at me before her mother grilled me then sped off. After a short drive we pulled up to what I believed to be a small holding facility. Led inside, I soon found out that I was going to questioned about the crime.

Placed in a room in which a mirror covered one wall, a table that had seen its days and two chairs, I sat and looked straight into the mirror. From watching all those cop shows, I knew that I was being watched. I wanted to shoot them the bird just to show them that I wasn't scared, but something stopped me short of doing so, likely because I was scared and didn't want them to beat me to death. I saw that in some movies.

After a while an investigator came in a sat across from me then asked what happened. At first, I wanted to lie, but elected to just tell him everything that I had done. I explained why I did it and how it wasn't supposed to happen as it did. Odd, but I felt a weight leave my shoulders once I was done. With me completed with my confession he left while telling me to sit tight. Despite my humiliation I had to smile because I knew that I wasn't going to be going anywhere for a while.

Leaning back in my chair my eyes drifted to the all-white ceiling as I realized that I was just like its color nothing. I know that they say that the color white is supposed to represent peace, purity, and tranquility, but when you look at that color or shade to be correct, you don't see anything, Now I believe that should be added to its definition because it's the truth. You look at a white wall and tell me what you see.

Back from my void though, an officer came in and escorted me out of the room and back into the squad car.

Jonah Sanders

Seated, I slumped over in defeat because I knew exactly where I was going, and no confession or repentance was going to change that. I was on my way to purgatory.

After about twenty minutes we pulled into the parking area then I was ushered inside. Taken into the intake area in which was full to capacity, I guess I wasn't the only one doing something stupid so early in the morning. Unhandcuffed, I was told to sit until my name was called.

Glancing around it seemed as if everyone had that "I didn't do it" look on their face. My peers were the base stereotypes: guys with dreadlocks and sagging pants, along with junkies. It was just a pathetic scene altogether. Why did I do something so stupid? I just couldn't fathom it as I sat with my head down.

I watched as people got into lines to use the phone. I thought about doing the same, but fought against it. Who was I going to call anyway? If I had someone to call, that I could rely on, then I wouldn't be in this mess in the first place. I thought about calling my grandmother, but shook that off as soon as it came, because I knew that if I told her what I had did, that she would probably have a heart attack.

As time passed an officer called me and took me out of the personal hell that I was feeling.

Being Arrested & Taken to Jail

Getting up, I was weighed, filled out some forms, then told to go sit back down until I was called again. Wait. Wait. Wait. I guess that since I had nothing to do I might as well wait.

After about an hour I was called again then led down a hall along with 15 other new intakes. We were taken to a large shower and told to wash with some soap that killed lice. Standing right next to each other, we stripped then washed quickly. Once done we were given uniforms and crocs to put on our feet. Now fully inmates, we were escorted to an elevator then taken to our assigned dormitories.

Myself and a few guys went into the same dormitories. I carried the little intake bag to my room that held sheets and hygienic items then sat on the steel toilet exhausted. Not seeing my cellmate, I assumed that he was off somewhere in the world of idiots, so I unpacked, made my bed then jumped under the covers. Trying to be tough, I mean mugged the blanket until I felt tears run down my cheeks as I cried myself to sleep.

Reflections on the Past

The life of a man upon earth is a warfare

-Job:7.1

Reflections on the Past

I was born September 17, 1986, in the city of Orange, New Jersey. My mother's name is Heather Ambrose and My father's name is Todd Sanders. Much of my childhood I can't recall, but I'll present what I can.

As a toddler I was raised by my mother in Newark, New Jersey. For those who don't know, Newark is one of the most populated cities in New Jersey with a huge Hispanic and black populous. Newark has been classified as one of the most dangerous cities in the United States due to street gangs, such as Bloods, Crips, and Latin Kings, so you can say that I was at disadvantage from the start. But, I remember us living with my mother's mother, my grandmother, Dorothy at one time. I recall the house always being full to capacity as numerous family members would frequent the halls at all the times of the day.

From there my mother moved us to the Westside of Newark, which at the time was the worst part of the city. Lonely and struggling, my mother began a relationship with a guy named David, in which is the brother of a famous singer. The problem with David was that he was extremely abusive. He was so abusive, that I remember one time when he came inside of the tiny one-bedroom apartment and accused my mother of something then beat her to a pulp. When that incident happened, I was about four or five years of age.

Jonah Sanders

It may be the grief and the power to suppress the pain of the past, but its hard for me to recall much from that time. I do recall living with my aunt, whom everyone called "Ricky." Most of the good memories that I have from that time come from her. They were minute, but compared to what I witnessed everyday living with my mother and the monster, it was pleasant. Sad as it sounds, but I always wished that my aunt was my mother.

My time with my aunt was short lived though; when one day my father came and picked me up as we went to the next city over, called East Orange. The house that I moved into was on 12 Maple Terrace, a four-bedroom located on a dead-end street that was filled with working class people. With the change of environment, I was culture shocked, I didn't see any junkies or prostitutes... it was nice and quiet. I didn't hear gun shots or loud music blasting.

People didn't mean mug you every time your looked at them; people on my street laughed and joked all the time.

My grandmother owned the home. Mrs. Alease Sanders was retired after working twenty long years as a janitor at Lincoln Elementary School. My father had served in the military, then became a firefighter for the city. Now, with the advancement in social standing I guess that everyone thinks things were "peachy" for me, but it wasn't. Living with my father and grandmother, the awkward thing was, that my grandmother was the one to raise me. My father and I lived in the same home, but never really did much together; there were times we did, but not much.

I believe it was because I honestly didn't understand my father. Mr. Todd Sanders was a handsome brown skin man of average height, fit and scholarly; it was just that... he acted white. He loved Rock & Roll music, preferred Howard Stern's Morning Show over the popular urban radio shows, watched Japanese animation, and well... was different. Everyone else in my neighborhood were the complete opposite; rocking to rap music, watching the typical ethnic shows and you know... just kicked it. With that being so I was torn between trying to be like my father or everyone else.

What made me shift to the crowd was when one day my father came into my room with a few sheets of notebook paper and a pen and told me to write the name on the top of the page on every line the name that I was born with, Jamir Kyle Ambrose was erased from history and Jonah Sanders was put in his place. If I can recall I was no more than 9 years old.

Jonah Sanders

I'm 100% sure that's when the rebellion started. In fact, that same night I had a dream the I'll never forget. In the dream I was laying on my back, but when I tried to move and speak, I couldn't as if something was holding my mouth and body down.

Waking up in a cold sweat I rocked in the bed afraid that something was coming to get me. Remembering the dream and how I called out for everyone, but with no one answering, I decided not to call anyone anymore. From that moment I begin to steal, talked back to my grandmother, skipped classes at school, I did everything. My punishment was always the same: whooping; no, I got abused.

My father would have me get naked and hold onto a Colum in the basement and beat me with a weight lifters belt until my grandmother would run in the basement demanding him to stop while screaming, "You're about to kill the boy!" I would feel so much pain that my screams would be heard in the neighbor's house. One day a friend of mine, who lived next door to me asked if I was alright. Not thinking nothing of it, I just replied, "I'm fine". Looking at me for a while, he told me that he heard me screaming.

Embarrassed and humiliated, I just dropped my head and without saying anything, walked into my grandmother's house and locked myself in my room. Sitting on the bed, I starred at the walls confused. Hate became the only emotion that I began to feel all the time. Then I had got word that I had a half-sister and a half-brother, so my hate was intensified I shut everyone out and continued to destroy myself by doing idiotic things.

But my grandmother tried, she really did. Every Sunday she forced me to go to church with her at Mount Olive Baptist Church, in which was pastored by Rev. Russell Fox. I went because I had to, but I'll be a liar if I state that I didn't like going sometimes. With the Evil Inside of me I just couldn't stop doing crazy stuff. I remember when I had once stolen out of the collection plate.

One day though, things took a dramatic change. I was about 12 years old when my father came into my room and told me that we were going for a ride. Not having any say so I went with him as he drove to the city of Orange, in which was only about ten minutes away. Parking in front of a huge building, my father told me to follow him inside. Inside, my father spoke to a receptionist as I waited patiently. Once he was done with his talk he turned to me, smiled, then said, "Always fight and don't let anyone mess with you", then walked out the building as I stood stuck I place.

Jonah Sanders

With about five minutes passed, a white man, in which whom name I can't remember, came to talk to me. This was one of the few times that I was around a white person. To be honest I can't recall ever seeing a white person in my city.

The only time that I did was when my father used to take me to the arcade and the mall.

The guy informed me that he was my DFACS counselor, then gave me five dollars to go across the street to Burger King and get something to eat. Not wanting to take it; my stomach got the best of me, so I took the money, purchased the food, then came back. Sitting down eating my food in his office, he watched me with weary eyes then told me that I was going to a Group Home once I finished eating. Confused, I asked him what exactly was a Group Home, then once told, I lost my appetite and tried to think clearly. Group Home?

"What about my grandmother?"

"Not...for a while at least, "he answered shaking his head sadly. Stunned-, I just sat there until he said that he was ready then we just got into his car. Once we began our trek across town I watched the cars pass and the people walking as I felt a sense of lost.

Reflections on the Past

Arriving at the Group Home, I was escorted inside then led to the room that I was about to share with another lost soul. All the other kids sized me up, likely because I was small, but I didn't care. The guy in charge informed me that he would talk to me tomorrow then he left me alone with all the other thrown of kids.

With the adults gone, I had two big kids come up to me asking me where I was from, but I didn't want to talk so I just ignored them. Clearly offended, the bigger of the two put his guard up. Remembering the last thing that my father told me, I hauled off in his face, knocking him out. No one wanted to talk anymore. What was there to talk about?

Laying in the bed I thought about my Grandmother as I reflected on all the stupidity that I had done. About a month later I was kicked out of the Group Home because I threw a kid through a wall; he had it coming. But my DFACS counselor picked me up and drove back to his office so that he could find me a new place to stay. Later, that evening I was placed in another Group Home in Plainfield, New Jersey.

Jonah Sanders

 I didn't stay there long so my counselor had to find me another place to stay.

The next place that I was located was in Southern, New Jersey. It was more of a family atmosphere because it was with a married couple, who were super Christian. I won't lie nor neglect to state it; they were fantastic people…. but strict. With them being Christian, everything was censored, I hated it. I began to sneak out at night and mess around in school. I honestly believe that I was just scared to admit that I liked the family.

I eventually left that home because I got caught stealing a bike. So, I was taken to my last Group Home, back in my hometown, that was called The Isiah House. Now, I must be honest and state that I learned a lot there because the director was like a big brother or uncle. He had us doing something every weekend. Living at The Isiah House was probably the best years of my young life because I learned various skills, primarily how to deal with numerous personalities as well as striving to be independent.

When I left there, I didn't do anything crazy; I just wanted to go live with my grandmother, whom took me in with open arms. My father had moved across town, so we didn't see each other, which was good, so it was just me and my grandmother living alone. Once I started to network on my own I dropped out of school and got a job at a record shop in Newark, then moved on to a job at Branch Brook Park Skating Rink because I wanted to be the DJ. I promoted teen parties and snuck into adult clubs and deejayed. I was intoxicated with music.

Everything was going well until one day, the guy that my grandmother was renting a room to came into the house and hung up the phone that I was using when I had left the room. With the guy seeing how irate I was he called the police and told them that I threated to kill him. I didn't but ran afraid of getting arrested. I slept in the streets, hungry and confused. Remembering that my aunt was in Atlanta with my mother, I took some money that I had then went to a guy who wanted to be my manager. Setting it up that I would live with one of his artist, I made my way down south letting the music guide me to an unknown place.

Being Convicted

Even in the depths of hell we must move on in hopes of reaching heaven.

-Jonah Sanders

Being Convicted

After Being housed in the County Jail for what seemed an eternity, I was seen I court. If I'm not mistaken, I had been in the county jail for about a year and a half. Numerous times I was called to court, but always set off and given another date. This had occurred seven or eight times, but what was the rush when I knew that I wasn't going anywhere but prison. My dormitory became my home away from home and my room a sanctuary.

I mainly stayed to myself, the same way that I had been in the streets, then with me being from out of state I just kept a low profile. This was easy because I was heavily medicated on psychotropic medication that had me sleep all the time. It was as if I was already dead. It was the same routine every day, so maybe the comparison of being dead is of killer, but... maybe a robot. Yeah...a robot.

Wake-up, eat, sleep, use the bathroom, eat, sleep. I'm sure that I was deeply depressed. I remember looking out of the window, through the bars that held me in, and look at the world that I once knew. When it was late I would just stare at the street lights, attracted to them as if I were a moth to a flame. At those times I would have to shake my head to clear the suicidal thoughts that plagued my mind.

Jonah Sanders

My mother would put money in my account, so I didn't have to starve to death. That was gladly accepted because I didn't eat much of what they fed because I had the conspiracy notion that they put stuff in the food, in attempt to control you. Maybe I was just trippin', but I still didn't eat it. So, with me being depressed and not eating I lost a lot of weight, but didn't care. It wasn't like I was going to the club or some grand event

I was stuck in a cell with a guy that smelled like gas and who talked about shooting people at random as well as having sex with any female that crossed his path. I mean any female literally. I was repulsed, but hey, I wasn't that much better, was I? Possibly, but I just blocked out reality and created my own world. Why not?

But I was finally called to court. Shackled up, I was escorted on the transfer bus, then within minutes we were off. The sun was barely up, and school students of my age were off to school. Wasn't that just me a year or so ago? I wanted to pull my face from the window, from the agony, but I couldn't. The sights, smells and sounds took over my entire being.

The ride over to the courthouse was short lived though, as we pulled into the underground parking deck. The other inmates and myself were ushered off the bus, unshackled, then placed in holding cells as we waited our turn to be called upon to see the judge. My mind drifted to another world as the medication that I was prescribed worked its magic. I felt as if I was flying. Most times.

A few hours passed when they had called my name, then I was escorted up an elevator to see my attorney. Making my way into a small cell that was made for attorney-client meetings, my attorney smiled at me as I sat then spoke fast about the deal that he reminded me of, a deal from a few months past was a sentence of fifteen years. I was reluctant at first, but had agreed to it. Placing the agreement in front of me to sign, I couldn't make out the words because I seemed as if the words were jumping off the page. My medication was working in overtime.

 Signing where he pointed at, he smiled at me then told me to hold tight. A few minutes later I was escorted into the courtroom then stood before the judge, who asked me a bunch of questions, in which I didn't understand. I was light headed and dizzy from the medication. I just answered "yes" or "no" when my lawyer told me to. My judge ranted and raved about it being Black History Month then stated that I had 30 years. Banging his gravel, I was escorted out of the courtroom confused.

Diagnostic

Now I know what cattle feels like.

-Jonah Sanders

Diagnostic

A few months passed after my conviction before I was told that I was about to be shipped to diagnostic. Instantly my stomach twisted and turned. Being in the county I had saw a few acts of violence, but not much. Blessed, my stay wasn't as bad as others that I was around. It may have been because the lot of us in the dorm were all somehow trying to wiggle out of getting a life sentence or executed. Being in the county gave you an illusionary belief that "possibly" some relief would come, but prison was a whole different story because you were already convicted.

Packing my meager belongings, I said my farewell to my cellmate, then made my way down the long hall, into an elevator, then finally shackled and placed on the bus for transport. There was about fifteen or sixteen of us that had seen each other before, but with the unknown looming ahead of us, we all sat with our own thoughts in silence. What was I thinking? I'm sure we all asked ourselves that questions as we hit the road as the nights darkness attempted to frighten us more. Fear was replaced with pure frustration and stupidity.

Here I was sixteen hours away from my home state on my way to prison. I didn't know anyone, so I knew that I didn't have any backing if I got into it with anyone;

so be it. Remembering what my father had told me when he had left me at the DFACS office those so many years ago, I held onto that as my only means to survival. They say that you'll find out what you're made of when faced with adversity, so I guess it was time for me to find out who and what I was.

With the bus rolling on I looked out of the window and watched as the city landscape turned into a country setting of tall trees and cow pastures. The sun began to rise making me hold my head down shamefully. When we made a stop, or slowed down and the cars next to us would look inside of the bus searching for answers. I wondered if we were all that different. Deep down I felt that we weren't.

After a while we rolled up to Georgia Diagnostic Prison in Jackson, Ga. Pulling up to the prison we waited in line behind a slew of other transport buses dropping off their newly convicted prisoners. Passing through one of the checkpoint after another we eventually pulled into its huge parking lot. I wasn't the only one in hell that day because my estimate, it was at least 600 guys walking around waiting to be transported. It was a crazy situation.

Diagnostic

Looking around, some of the guys joked as if being in prison wasn't a big deal. Others mean mugged everyone they looked at, I even saw a bunch of homosexuals gathering around each other giggling. I couldn't believe where I was at and saw. Close your eyes and imagine it.

Parking the bus driver instructed us to Stay seated until he came back. (Like we could go anywhere) Returning within minutes with the officer that had rode with him in the front, they opened the cage that separated us then instructed us to come out one by one so that we could be unshackled. We all stood to stretch our legs and made our way off unshackled, I looked at everyone around me to make sure no one could just walk up on me. I knew that I didn't have any enemies, but I wasn't taking any chances.

Placing my back on the bus I watched everyone talk and walk around. Time passed, then the driver called out our names. Everyone stopped what they were doing and paid attention, so they would know where they would be going to be permanent out. I just wanted to get the whole ordeal over with, so I could try to figure out a way to get out of my situation. Finally, I was called and instructed to go over to another bus to board. Re-shackled. Then placed on the bus we were told that we were going to another diagnostic prison called Coastal State Prison.

Jonah Sanders

After a few hours of driving we pulled up to the prison. Going through the same routine of sitting, being shackled, then ushered off the bus, the lot of us were taken to the intake section of the prison, and of course, told to wait some more. Stripped, we were told to take a shower with some liquid soap. After a quick wash, we were all give a pair of boxers, undershirt, socks and jump suit. Finished with that we were each given a bag that held a bar of soap, roll of toilet tissue, toothbrush, toothpaste, deodorant, two bed sheets, a blanket, pillow case, two pairs of socks, two undershirts, two boxers and another jumpsuit. Once everyone received their bags we were escorted to medical so that we all could do a physical.

Completed with that part of humiliation we were finally taken to our dormitory. Walking in a straight line we moved fast because we were all tired. At the dorm we were told which bed was ours out of the twenty-five bunkbeds. Dead tired from the long ride, thinking too hard, and being ordered what to do. I made my bed and watched everyone as I laid on top on the covers. With sleep over taking me I dreamed of freedom.

Diagnostic

For the next few months I had to do numerous test ranging from I.Q to physical. The time droned on as I got my first taste of slavery. Now, don't get me wrong, being in the County you had a sense of slavery, but once you were convicted, it got real. In prison you had to be in a straight line everywhere; you were given a job that didn't pay you, then you were told when you could speak.

There were daily inspections of your bunk and locker in which you had to stand ramrod straight as the warden walked around. But if I thought that diagnostics was bad I was seriously mistaken when I went to my first permanent prison.

Prison Beginnings

Helpless in a void. Could I be someone when I lived as if I were nothing?

-Jonah Sanders

Prison Beginnings

Early on a Monday morning I was told to pack up and that I was transferring to my permanent prison. Getting out of the bed, I packed up my property – slowly. What was the rush? It wasn't like I was going anywhere I wanted. I had 30 odd years to do in the state pen.

I was depressed and didn't care about anything, so I took my time to pack up; they could wait. But, even with me moving as slow as I could I completed the task then made my way to be shipped off with the other slaves. What made my dispositions worst was when the driver told us that we were going to Hays State Prison. Great. The first prison that I was going to be housed in was one of the worst in the nation.

My pulse quickened as I thought about how I was going to make up. I was eighteen, slim, considered a "pretty boy" and had no backing. My mind raced back to what my old cellmate in the county told me, to stab the first person who looked at me wrong. Yeah, that's what ill do. With me having so much time I was going to gain respect…. yeah, I'll stab someone.

I was already in prison so there wasn't much they could do to me, right? Comforted by the notion that I would stab someone if they got wrong with me, I sat back with a grin.

Jonah Sanders

What would you be thinking if you were in my position? I just wanted to survive.

With the sun rising we pulled up at the Georgia Diagnostic Prison after a four and a half drive, so that I could be placed on another bus, that would take me to Hays State Prison. Stepping off the bus I stretched my limb and let my eyes scan the huge parking lot, taking in all the busses and inmates. It was as if it was its own world, because everything was totally different from what I was used to before I was arrested. Even with things being restricted it still had its own pace of things; somewhat like an old impala on the road with a Porsche. You can say it was like being in a world that is transparent.

With my mind wondering I became frustrated, but also fascinated with this new world that I was in, so I began walking around watching how people communicated. Some looked friendly while you had others with the whole hard convict look. I wondered how I looked to some of the guys around me. After a few laps around the lot I stood by the bus that I had rode on then waited until I was instructed on what to do next. About thirty minutes later I was told to go to a bus across the lot.

Picking up my property I made my way over to my next transport, giving my name, I placed my property on the side of the bus then got re-shackled as

Prison Beginnings

I got onto the bus. Everyone looked pissed off because we were going to Hays; I couldn't blame them either. Sitting down I prayed that it wouldn't be too bad. After riding for about three hours we pulled up to the prison.

Soon as we pulled in officers wearing all black came out to meet us. Once we were all unshackled we were told to face the wall and not to speak. Then out of no where I heard someone screaming in my ear.

"Now listen you no good piece of crap! You're in our world now and we don't care how bad you were in the streets! We run this! Now, if you do as your told then we won't have to break you in half! Understand?"

I felt like my eardrum was about to bust. Honestly, I was more annoyed then scared. I replied that I understood then waited for him to back up. I guess that he was satisfied with my answer because he moved away from me then screamed to everyone, "Good! Very good! Now let's get moving! Its time that you all get into your dorms."

Following behind him into the intake area, all our property was searched to see if any of us had any contraband: knives, phones, money, etc. Once that was done each one of us had to go behind a curtain and get stripped search, spreading your butt cheeks, squatting and coughing, just humiliating stuff. Feeling less than human, we were then each given an intake package that was identical to the one that I was given in diagnostic. I guess it was its own Hotel.

Ushered out of the intake area into the main compound I got my first glimpse of real prison life. Funny, but the first thing that I saw were guys playing a softball game. Ruefully, it reminded me of the movie "Life" that stared Eddie Murphy and Martin Lawrence. Guys looked as if that didn't have a worry in the world. I had to shake my head as I tried to comprehend how people could be so happy in prison. All my way to the dormitory I pondered on that.

Once at my dormitory I carried my stuff inside and made my way to my assigned room. Stepping through the sally port, the first thing I saw was a guy on the phone. Nodding his way in a form of a greeting, I looked at the other guys that were in the day area. The ages ranged from young and old, but they all were doing the same thing; nothing. You had a few guys playing chess, a few working out, but everyone else was just lounging around.

Placing my stuff into my room, I made my bed then placed a few belongings in my locker. The room consisted of a bunkbed, in which the bedframe was smaller than one at a cheap hotel, a steel toilet, steel sink… that's it.

Prison Beginning

This was the place that I was to be for a few decades. In the back of the room was a window that was caged, but I stood by it trying to get some fresh air. I stood there until someone knocked on my door and said, "What's up."

Turning his way, I just looked at my visitor without speaking, then gave him a nod in greeting. He was an old black inmate that was stooped over so I didn't take him as a threat.

"Where you from?"

"Jersey," I replied, not wanting to talk, but I knew that this was going to happen, so I just wanted to get it out of the way. My old cellmate in the county had told me when I made it to prison someone would come to me and ask a few questions to get the run down on me. He had gone on explaining that it was important to build a rapport with people in the joint. So here I was waiting. I really wanted him to hurry up. "So, What you in for?"

Doing better than merely answering, I pulled out the list of my charges and handed it to him. He looked over it quickly then whistled. Satisfied or whatever, he said "Oh, you'll be fine." Handing me the list back, "Names Ole 'school and I'm the one who runs things here. We just don't like sex offenders; thank God, you're not one because it would have been a prison. You need anything?"

"I'm from Jersey. I don't need anyone's help period." Looking across at me, Ol'school nodded to himself then said, "Yeah, you'll be alright," then left out leaving me to my window as I went back to thinking – hard.

Later that day, I found out who my bunkmate was; a dark skin guy who called himself Black who was from South Carolina. Black worked in the prisons laundry room washing everyone's dirty boxers or what not. When he told me that he worked in the laundry he made it seem as if it was one of his greatest accomplishments in life; pathetic, right? Annoyed, I asked him how much he got paid. He got silent then said that the prison didn't pay him, but he hustled and made money by charging people to be their laundry man, in which consisted of him bleaching their clothes and pressing it.

I had to stifle a laugh because I couldn't understand working for free, then couldn't fathom why guys would pay someone to do their laundry when the prison did it anyway. I understood that guys may have wanted to have their clothes bleached and pressed, but for what? It wasn't like we all had somewhere important to go.

Prison Beginning

It all seemed stupid to me. Think about it, what sense did it make?

Seeing that I wasn't impressed with his vocation, Black went on and told me that I was going to get a job too; likely in the kitchen. I laughed right in his face at that. Me, work for free; not happening. That was slavery. But my bunkmate may have had the last laugh because later that week I was assigned to the kitchen to work the morning shift.

At 2 A.M my door clicked then I was told that I was to clean pots and pans. Getting up and then making my way inside of the kitchen I was appalled when I saw so many roaches; along with more than a few rats. Guys were playing in their noses and wiping buggers on the wall; it was crazy. When I was taken to the area to wash the pots and pans, I refused; I couldn't do it. What could they do to me.?

Well, I found out as they took me to the lockdown unit. Being housed into a cell by myself was to be punishment for not working, plus a disciplinary report that costed me five dollars. So, I was to be locked in a room for 24 hours a day for not working; so be it. It gave me time to think of a way on how to get out of my situation.

Jonah Sanders

Talking to an officer I found out that the prison had a library that provided legal books for people who wanted their case, so I gained from not working.

Within a week I was released from lockdown and placed back in general population. Once out I was assigned back to the kitchen. So, I refused again. This went on for about five times until they realized that I wasn't going to work. I stayed in the dormitory and read the legal books trying to understand something. I was lost at what I was reading, but I knew that I had to figure something out.

Violence

Ignorance can make a man become enraged. Fear can make a man violent.

-Jonah Sanders

Violence

Years passed with the constant feeling of non-existence. The constant demand to work for free was annoying, then I realized that many of the people around me were content with their confides. This was obvious because when I would look around the usual routines for most was to get up, work, shower, eat, watch television, go back to sleep to start the cycle all over again. It was much to bear, but I pushed on. All I had was myself, so I had to fight to keep my mind focus despite the feeling that the entire world was against me.

The prison was making a change, especially when tobacco products were taken out of the system. So, whenever someone could get it, either by smuggling it in through visitation, paying an officer to bring it in, or having it thrown over the fence, they were king of the land. A measuring cup of tobacco went for $50; sometimes $100 if it was slack. Then younger inmates came into the prison system introduced an influx of gangs. If I can recall, the year of 2008 was the beginning of the rise in violence.

Some people blamed the system because they took lunch away on Fridays leaving inmates to only receive three meals a day Monday thru Thursday. Others blamed the President of the United States for passing the

Jonah Sanders

 Bill that took away tobacco, but it was neither. All you had to do was look at the mind state of most prisoners. When the lunch was taken away on Friday's guy just laid down and went for it. True enough, some cried about it, but it was basically ignored as if it wasn't a big deal.

But look at what happened a few years after tobacco was outlawed. You had sit downs proposed demanding that we get tobacco back. Why wasn't anyone coming together so that guys got paid for work? Basically, every other state was getting paid. What about how bad the food was?

With the objective of this chapter being on violence I'll move on, but just think about how dumb these guys are. In my prison stay I witnessed a few acts of violence, but the worst that I saw was when I was transferred to Telfair State Prison. As the transport bus pulled up to the prison I got a bad feeling immediately. My breathe quickened as my heart beat hard in my chest, so I knew that something was definitely wrong. I wasn't scary, but it just didn't feel right.

I wasn't the only one who felt it because guys that were in a deep conversation stopped and got into a meditative silence. Telfair State Prison had a name for its violence, but sitting in its parking lot it was intense. After a while I got myself together then made my way off the bus and got unshackled. I had been in the system for a while, so I had built a reputation of someone who stayed to himself, but would handle a situation if it presented itself, so I knew a few guys that had my back if something went down; hopefully nothing would happen though.

With everyone off the bus, we marched inside to get striped searched and have our property searched. Once done with that we had to go to medical for a quick check, then told which dormitory that we were assigned to. Given my intake packet I was told that I was going to the lockdown unit with three other guys because there weren't any beds available in general population. I don't know if I was relieved or what, but I almost hugged the officer. Out of the intake area then onto the main compound everyone was hit with the feel of death.

I knew that I wasn't the only one who felt if because everyone stopped and looked at each other with wide eyes. As I scanned the compound it looked out of control. In other prisons, inmates had to walk inside of a line that was painted on the ground, here everyone was grouped up in gangs. It seemed as if no one walked alone. As I stated earlier, the gangs had taken over the prison system, so scary guys jumped at the chance to join whichever would accept them. Honestly, I thought most of them were cowards.

You had Bloods, Crips, Gangster Disciples, Arian Nation, but the worst were the Goodfellas. It didn't matter if it was just two of them, they would go to war with thirty if they had to. A lot of gangs didn't like the Goodfellas, but they sure didn't want to go to war with them. The second most dangerous group were the Spanish. They didn't bother anyone, but when it went down they were trying to kill something.

Once myself and the other guys walked into the lockdown unit all you could here was, "Ca-Rip! Blaat! GD! MOB!" it was crazy. I guess they wanted to let whoever was coming in know that they weren't alone if they were in a gang. I personally believe that guys just wanted to start a new beginning and be a part something, so they just got into a gang in a way to replace their family that they lost. I could be wrong, but I doubt it. Growing up I had dabbed in the gang life and that's why I got in to it. What do you think?

Ushered to my room, I walked in as the door slammed hard behind me then immediately heard my neighbor

Violence

call me through the vent.

"Who that be?"

Not wanting to talk, but being respectful and understanding that this was all apart of Prison, I replied, "J."

"You Blood?"

"Nope."

"You got love for Blood?"

"I love everyone. What's up?"

"Just seeing what was going on. It's a war zone out there."

Not replying to that, I meditated on the last thing he said. Great! I just got transferred to a prison that was in the middle of a gang war. Unpacking my property, I laid down and drifted off to sleep as I continued to hear the gang calls as if they were dogs howling at the moon. It was what it was.

About a week had went by when I was told to pack my stuff up that I was going to general population. One thing about prison was that guys would talk about everything and everyone, so if you were smart all you had to do was listen. Carrying my property out of the dorm

Jonah Sanders

I placed it in a cart knowing exactly what was going on in the prison, so felt a little better.

 "What dorm you going to?" A guy that had got out of lockdown asked.

"H building."

"Oh, that's the new building in the b ack. Ain't nothing going on back there; you straight."

I was relieved to hear that, but didn't show it. I was about to say something, but stopped short when I looked on the yard and saw a group charging another screaming, "Mob!" The other was ready though as they pulled out shanks and stabbed the oncoming group. Our escort officer ran onto the yard as other officers made their way to try to stop the war. The officers sprayed pepper spray and some tear gas until everyone got on the ground, but they were too late because on of the guys were dead from a stab wound in his neck.

Loneliness

Have you ever felt as lonely as me?

-Jonah Sanders

Loneliness

Violence out of the way, in which my opinion, the most unbearable thing about prison is the loneliness that one feels. Honestly, I believe that's one of the main reasons why guys are so violent; just another way to express their pain. At times I wanted to lash out at whoever was close to me, but I would catch myself and remember that they weren't the one that I was angry with, but my own stupidity. It was tough.

Some nights when I would have time to myself I would have to hold back tears of frustration. Thoughts of my childhood would come to mind and I would shrink deeper inside of myself as I would remember my grandmother waking me up for church or when we would have family get togethers at my cousin, Shelia's. I would be able to taste all my favorite foods and hear all the songs that I used to listen to. But my time got even worst when my mother died. I remember being called to the Chief Counselors office and told the sad news.

At first, I tried to act as if it wasn't a big deal and that I had lost any feelings of love and compassion, but as I walked out of the office my legs gave out from up under me as I began to cry uncontrollably. Her death took me through a loop so much to the point where I contemplated suicide. My mother and I didn't even know each other well, but she was all I had.

Jonah Sanders

I thought of numerous way to end my life.

 I just couldn't take it anymore. Slicing my wrist didn't seem logical. I had saw plenty guys try to end their life that way, but it didn't work. Trying to hang myself came to mind, but the thought passed as fast as it came. I got depressed at one time that I even asked the medical department to give me some pills so that I wouldn't wake up. I couldn't take being in prison anymore.

Constantly being talked down to by staff, having to watch my back for potential enemies, not having anything to do, then being alone seemed to much. Some guys went to church or to Islamic services, but it was mainly "chain gang religion." One day they were stabbing someone for something petty then the next they would call everyone for prayer. It was all a joke to me. Think about it.

I did dab in Islam because when I was twelve I had converted to the religion, but felt that it was too much like a gang.

Guys who take up Arabic names, wear kufis, then feel self-righteous. Funny thing was that the same individuals were the ones who stayed in nonsense. Now, I wasn't a religious expert, but I remember the Muslims that I grew up around and they didn't act anything like what I witnessed in prison.

Loneliness

The ones that I remembered were peaceful and strived to practice what they taught.

Some guys would write to pen pals or do some type of arts & crafts. I tried the pen pal thing, but didn't like it because what I really wanted was to connect with my family. True, when I was a child I was out of control, but I had learned from my errors. Being so far away from home all the friends that I once had were long gone. I became ashamed and felt like a failure. I would think about my grandmother and drop my head as I realized how I had let her down.

I let everyone down, but Importantly I let myself down. Feeling hopeless I would just sleep the days away. It was as if I was one of the Walking Dead. What else was I to do, plus everyone else was doing it. Why did I have to be different? I had no hope and believed that I was stuck in hell.

Breaking the Chains

If I don't fight what enslaves me, not only just physically, but also mentally and emotionally I will always be shackled.

-Jonah Sanders

Breaking the Chains

One night I had a dream that changed my life. I was on a boat inside of a torch lit tunnel. The individual who commanded the boat had an old Chinese peasants hat along with a long red garb. The face of the individual was hard to see due to the gloom of the tunnel, but it seemed disfigured. Silently, we moved along the waters.

At first, I was to shock to speak, but curiously got the best of me when I asked where we were going. The commander of the boat just pointed straight; revealing a skeletal hand. Not knowing what to say or do I just sat back and waited to see where I was going. Odd as it may sound, but I felt that I was going to hell. It may be hard to believe, but I wasn't scared. I assumed that it was my fate. My life was basically over with; I was alone and wanted to die anyway.

Coming to the opening of the tunnel, I was surprised to see grass on both sides of me. The sun shined as I realized that I was in a garden. Moving along we stopped in front of a waterfall, then a loud voice called out "Live!" waking up in my bed I couldn't do anything, but sit silently as I looked around my room. With my eyes stopping on the bible and Quran that I had laying in my locker.

I laughed out loud.

Jonah Sanders

I knew both books rather well, but never actually chose which to follow. Feeling as if my body was on fire I blacked out. Coming to, I thought about the people in the world that needed help then thought about Malcolm X and Nelson Mandela. At first not understanding it I caught on that I needed to forget about my own pain and frustration and fight for others who weren't capable of bearing it. There was so much injustice in the world; so much that needed to be fixed.

...So, I decided to do what I could to help out.

Appendix 1

Understanding Ethics

"Good people do not need laws to tell them to act responsibly, while bad people will find a way around the laws."

-Plato

Appendix 1: Understanding Ethics

One of the most important things that must be established for your growth is that you have ethics. Due to the fact that some of you may not know what ethics are, I will present its definition so that you can adequately follow this lesson.

The American Heritage Dictionary defines ethics as: <u>the study of the general nature morals and of the specific moral choices to be made by a person as well as the rules or standards governing the conduct of a person or members of a profession.</u>

Simply put, ethics are what we define as right and wrong. Understand? Alright, here is a scenario that I want you to consider-honestly. There is no right or wrong answer because this is only to be a reflective glance as to where you are on an ethical level.

You are walking down the street and see an older woman who is screaming that her purse was just snatched by a robber. Not only does the woman scream that her purse was taken, but that it contained her money that covered her rent. Later, that day a friend of yours comes around and brags about robbing an older woman earlier that day. What do you do?

As I've stated already, there is no right or wrong answer, just your honest answer.

Jonah Sanders

Remember that you cannot have any personal growth unless you're honest with yourself. I'll ask these though:

What factors did you consider when making the decision?

Did you consider that she was a woman?

Was it because it was her rent money?

What was it?

Matter of fact, I'll present another scenario so that you can reflect more on yourself.

You are at school and get into it with a group of individuals who hurt you badly. Time passes, and you see one of the people that had hurt you; only this time you're with your friends.

In the back of your mind you want revenge, but then one of your friends pulls out a gun and points it at the person. What do you do now?

Again, there is no right or wrong answer – just your honest one. Deep down your integrity and values will make your decision. What level of integrity do you have? What do you value? What are your morals?

When you have answered the above questions, now

Appendix 1: Understanding Ethics

it's time to understand the levels of ethical Issues. The two Main ethical issues that you will face are:

Societal Issues

At the societal level you must question the institutions in a society. For example: Are north Koreans ethically correct for threatening the world with nuclear weapons? Some of you may think that this doesn't play a part in your everyday life, but it does.

Personal Issues

These are the day-to-day questions that occur in everyday situations. This is simply the question of how to treat people around you.

Now, some unethical behaviors may lead people to financial or some other benefit, but the consequences may range from the feeling of guilt in which would destroy them from inside out. Think about something that you've done that your regret. We all have something that we regret so don't act like you don't. A good study to follow is: If you have any doubt about something leave it alone because its likely wrong.

Jonah Sanders

Before you decide, think about if your choice will affect your image or if it puts a knot in your stomach. So, if you are serious with this lesson you'll have a good start.

Appendix 2

Looking into the Mirror

"If you never find out who you are then you're nothing but a poltergeist whose being is lost and at odds with universal law"

-Jonah Sanders

Appendix 2: Looking into the Mirror

Simple question: Who are you? Go ahead and take a moment to think about it. Look at who you are physically, emotionally, intellectually, and spiritually. Do you like who you are? Do you wish to advance in some of those aspects?

These are the reflective glances that will help you get where you want to be in life, but you must first know who you are. Through ignorance we, yes, we, fail to take the necessary steps to push forward and accomplish all that we want out of life. So, after you reflect on who you are, the next thing for us to look at is how to get where you want to be.

So, how do you get to your destination in life?

1. Experience that "light bulb moment." That moment when you suddenly realize what you want out of life and how to get it.
2. Take counsel from someone who cares about and knows the "real" you, not the image that you at times put on as a smoke screen. Get a mentor, friend, teacher, or religious leader and have them point you to your destination.
3. Take your time to learn as much as you can so that your ride to your destination is a smooth as possible. You can easily learn from others and generalized studies.

Getting to your destination may not be easy.

- You may have to do more reflection.
- You may not like what you see in yourself.
- You may have the wrong destination in mind.
- You may have to sacrifice something.

If you really want to reach your destination you can't let anything get in your way; you must fight with all your might for a place in the world then hold onto it and guard it with your life. To get where you want, you to have to keep it in mind 24 hours a day until you attain it.

A few examples of individuals who fought against opposition until they reached their destination are:

Shawn "Jay -Z" Carter, who was born and raised in the tough projects in Brooklyn, NY. Despite being in an environment that placed his back against the wall he has become one of the most influential people in the world.

Albert Einstein. As a child he was considered slightly retarted. Unfazed, his mother placed him through home school. Later in life, he became one of the greatest scientist to ever walk the planet.

Appendix 2: Looking into the Mirror

Michael Jordon was cut by his high school basketball team. Despite the opposition he continued to work with the team anyway, then eventually made the team the following year. We all know that he became arguably the best player in the history of basketball, but what if he had just quit?

To conclude, I humbly ask that you write a blueprint describing where you are in life, what you want out of it, and how you're going to get it.

About the Author

Born and raised in Northern New Jersey, Jonah Sanders is a poet, author, brand manager and social activist. For those that wish to Follow or Contact him you may do so on: insidethemindofjonahsanders.com

©